Water
for
the
World

By Franklyn M. Branley

COLOR: FROM RAINBOWS TO LASERS

COMETS, METEOROIDS, AND ASTEROIDS:

  MAVERICKS OF THE SOLAR SYSTEM

THE EARTH: PLANET NUMBER THREE

THE ELECTROMAGNETIC SPECTRUM

ENERGY FOR THE 21ST CENTURY

EXPERIMENTS IN SKY WATCHING

EXPERIMENTS IN THE PRINCIPLES OF SPACE TRAVEL

FEAST OR FAMINE? THE ENERGY FUTURE

LODESTAR: ROCKET SHIP TO MARS

MAN IN SPACE TO THE MOON

MARS: PLANET NUMBER FOUR

THE MILKY WAY: GALAXY NUMBER ONE

THE MOON: EARTH'S NATURAL SATELLITE

THE NINE PLANETS

PIECES OF ANOTHER WORLD: THE STORY OF MOON ROCKS

SOLAR ENERGY

THE SUN: STAR NUMBER ONE

Water
for
the
World

by
Franklyn M.
Branley

illustrated by
True Kelley

T.Y. Crowell New York

Library of Congress Cataloging in Publication Data

Branley, Franklyn Mansfield, 1915–
Water for the world.

Summary: Discusses the sources of the world's water
supply, methods of getting water from its source to
where it's needed, the dangers of pollution, and the need
for conservation.
1. Water-supply—Juvenile literature. 2. Hydrology—
Juvenile literature. [1. Water supply. 2. Water]
I. Kelley, True, ill. II. Title.
TD348.B7 1982   333.91   81-43321
ISBN 0-690-04172-1   AACR2
ISBN 0-690-04173-X (lib. bdg.)

1 2 3 4 5 6 7 8 9 10
First Edition

Contents

1 | The Water Cycle

Every day each of us uses about 90 gallons of water. The largest amount—32 gallons—is used for washing and cleaning ourselves, our clothes, our dishes, and our homes. Twenty-five to 30 gallons are used for flushing the toilet; 25 to 30 gallons go into swimming pools and onto lawns; and about two gallons are used for drinking and cooking.

If you multiply 90 gallons by the number of people in our country, the total is close to a staggering 20 billion gallons. But that's just a small part of the total amount of water that America uses every day. We use water to irrigate our farms and to keep our factories operating. It takes 120 gallons of water to produce one egg—that is, when you count the amount needed to grow the food for the hen, and the water the hen drinks. It takes about 3,500 gallons of water to produce a pound of steak; 21 gallons to make a gallon of gasoline; and almost 60,000 gallons to manufacture a ton of steel. When all these uses of water are added together, the amount America uses adds up to almost 500 billion gallons every day!

The wonder is that so much water flows out of our faucets—and there always seems to be more if it should be needed. We are fortunate; only in our country, and in Canada and Europe, is good drinking water abundantly available. In other parts of the world, water has to be carried in buckets, and much of that water is not pure. It often carries disease and is otherwise unpleasant to drink.

Water for our daily needs comes from rivers and lakes or from reservoirs, which are man-made lakes. It also comes from vast stores under the ground. (Groundwater lodges in layers of rocks, sand and soil.) For water to be useful, it must not contain salt—that is why we can't use ocean water. It must also be free of substances that would be harmful to us, such as bacteria and certain chemicals.

The water cycle purifies our water and renews the supply. Here is how the water cycle works. Rain falls into lakes and streams, and we use that water in the ways mentioned earlier. The used water goes into the ground, or into a sewage system. The water may then flow back into lakes and streams, and some of it evaporates into the air. Water also evaporates from the oceans, from trees and plants, from animals, and from you and me. It goes into the air as water vapor, a colorless, odorless, dry gas.

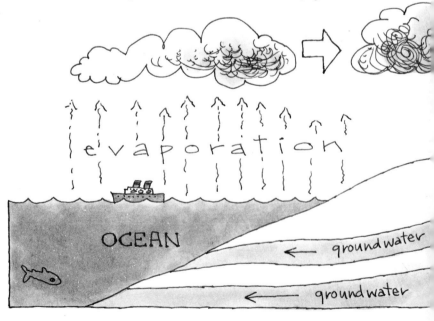

When water vapor cools, it condenses into water droplets so small that 100,000 of them could be contained in an ordinary drop. These droplets join together to make clouds. Winds blow the clouds from place to place. When the concentration of water droplets becomes great enough, the droplets form drops, and they fall as rain. The water may fall as snow when temperatures are low.

When water evaporates, impurities are left behind. They do not evaporate. When rain falls, the water may pick up a few impurities from the air, but usually it will remain quite clean and pure. The water will once again be suitable for use in our homes, for irrigating, and for industry.

Water is used over and over again. The water you drink today was here in the days of the dinosaurs, and long before that. It is made of the same molecules—it is water that has been evaporating, condensing into droplets, and then raining down on the earth over and over again for several billion years.

Usually the water cycle can be relied upon to renew *America's* water. That's because rain falls every so often throughout the year, so lakes and streams are refilled. But sometimes there are droughts —long periods of no rainfall—and the water level in lakes and rivers gets lower and lower. Then people go on water emergency —they must use less water so the supply is not exhausted entirely.

Water emergencies may also occur if many people are concentrated in an area where there are few lakes and reservoirs. In northern New Jersey, for example, there are many cities and towns. During the winter, rain and snow collect in the area's reservoirs, often filling them completely. But the reservoirs cannot hold enough water to carry northern New Jersey through a drought that may occur in summer or fall. When the reservoirs are drained, other sources of water must be found. This happened in 1980 –81, when there was little or no rain for several months. In this emergency, pipes carried water from lakes elsewhere in the state to the northern New Jersey reservoirs. But this was not a happy solution, because if too much water was piped out, the lakes would be drained. And these lakes are lined with summer cottages —they are recreation centers, and the people who live there need the water for their own use.

One solution to northern New Jersey's water problem would be to build more reservoirs. Another solution would be to build long pipelines to carry water from lakes at far-off locations. That's what New York City has done. Every day the city uses one and a half billion gallons of water. Huge pipes called aqueducts carry the water for 100 miles or more from a series of lakes and reservoirs in upper New York State. California gets a lot of its water the same way. California pipes in water from the Colorado River, and also from reservoirs in the mountains east of the state. A network of aqueducts distributes the water. People in New Jersey, New York, and California hope for heavy snows in the winter, for when heavy snows melt, they fill the reservoirs. The water emergency in New Jersey continued until late spring in 1981 when heavy rains filled the reservoirs.

If there were fewer people in the world, fewer farms that needed to be irrigated, and fewer industries, the water cycle could be relied upon for a steady supply of good water. But populations have become larger, so farms have had to produce more food and industry has had to make more products. (Farmers now irrigate 60 million acres—each one requiring thousands of gallons of water each growing season.) The need for water has skyrocketed, so people have sought ways to keep the water supply at a high level.

11

Two million dams have been built to hold back water—to keep it from flowing away. And millions upon millions of wells have been dug to bring groundwater to the surface. In Houston, Texas, so much water has been pumped out of the ground that the ground has sunk. In many places houses have sunk also, and people have had to move out of them.

When water becomes scarce, people suddenly realize how important it is. Life cannot continue without a supply of good water; every plant and animal needs it. Without water, a town or even an entire region becomes a wasteland. Imagine what a calamity it would be if your city, town, or village had no water—if you turned on the faucet and no water came out!

Like the air we breathe, good, clean water is an essential re-source. When we have it, we don't think much about where it comes from, or how fragile the supply really is.

There is a limited amount of water on our planet. In this book we'll see where the water we use comes from, that only a small percentage of it can be used, and how important it is for each of us to use water with care.

2 | Oceans, Glaciers, and Icebergs

You may live in a place where water is always available—all you have to do is turn on a faucet and there it is. But this is not true in most parts of the world. Rainfall in much of Asia, Africa, Australia, and in much of Western United States is not enough to meet people's needs. Besides that, there are few lakes, rivers, or reservoirs, and wells are far apart. In some parts of Africa people must walk ten miles a day to fetch a jar of water.

Although there is a tremendous amount of water on our planet, very little of it is usable. Over 97 percent of the water on earth is in oceans. It is salt water, so it cannot be used for drinking, cooking, washing, or irrigating, or in manufacturing. Less than 3 percent of the world's water is fresh (free from salt). Two-thirds of this fresh water is frozen in glaciers and ice caps. In fact, less than 1 percent of earth's water supply can be used. This is the water in rivers and lakes, and groundwater within about half a mile of earth's surface.

Ocean water can be made usable by removing the salt. That is now being done in a few places. One of these places is Kuwait, a country on the Persian Gulf that has no fresh water source. Seawater is heated and evaporated in a series of boilers, and then the water vapor is condensed. In the process, salts are gradually removed and the water becomes fresh.

Producing fresh water by this method is very expensive because so much fuel is required to heat the seawater. Kuwait can afford to do it because it has abundant oil supplies, and the highest income per person in the world. Kuwait's plant produces over 15 million gallons of fresh water a day.

An efficient way of getting fresh water from seawater is to use waste heat from electric generating stations. The steam needed to run turbines is heated to a very high temperature—750 to 950 degrees Fahrenheit. When the steam leaves the turbines, it is still very hot—well over 212°, the boiling point. This heat can be used

to heat seawater. The hot seawater then goes into a chamber where the pressure is lower than air pressure. Because of the lower pressure, the seawater evaporates at once—this is called flash evaporation. Next the vapor condenses; then the liquid goes into another chamber where the pressure is even lower. Once again the water evaporates and then condenses. There may be a series of as many as 30 or 40 chambers—each successive one at a lower pressure. In each chamber some of the salts in the water are left behind, so in the end there is fresh water.

This method of converting salt water to fresh water is used in Kuwait and on some desert islands. (One is Aruba, off the coast of South America.) And eventually California will make fresh water this way, using waste heat from nuclear generating stations. Meanwhile, people in other areas of the world are experimenting with other ways of increasing their fresh water supplies.

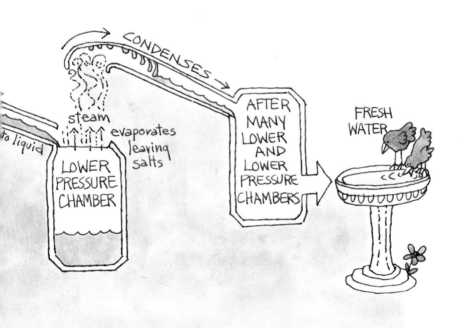

Solar Evaporators

Solar evaporators are now being tested in Chile and Israel, on some Greek islands, and in several Arab countries—places that have ample sunshine and limited fresh water sources. The evaporators are used in a process called solar distillation. The process is a way of converting salt water to fresh water without expensive fuel for heating the salt water.

A device that will remove salt from water by using solar energy can be made with a carton, a coffee can, and pieces of plastic film.

cut out
window

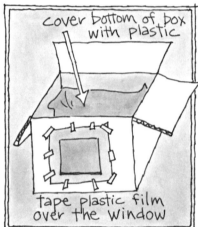

cover bottom of box
with plastic

tape plastic film
over the window

Cut a large window near the bottom of one side of a cardboard carton, preferably one that is square. Tape a sheet of plastic film over the window. Cover the bottom of the box with a large sheet of plastic. (You might use a dry-cleaners bag.) Then set a coffee can in the center of the bottom of the box. Cut a sheet of plastic large enough to cover the top of the box *after* the center of the plastic has been pushed down to the can.

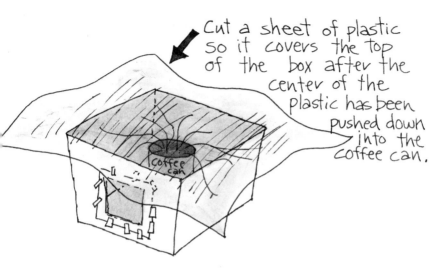

Cut a sheet of plastic so it covers the top of the box after the center of the plastic has been pushed down into the coffee can.

coffee can

To operate your evaporator, you'll need water, salt, and a towel. Mix up a batch of salty water. Then soak the towel in it. Wring out some of the water but leave the towel very wet, just dry enough so it doesn't drip.

SALT

WATER

Soak a towel in salty water.

Wring it out so it's very wet but doesn't drip.

Arrange the wet towel around the can on the plastic in the bottom of the box. Tape the precut piece of plastic over the top of the carton, pushing the center of it down to the can. A small rock will hold the plastic in place over the can and will tighten the plastic. If you wish, cover the box with a piece of cardboard.

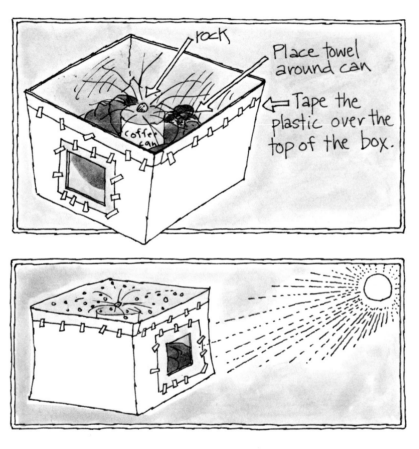

Place the evaporator in sunlight so the sun shines through the window and onto the towel. Water will evaporate from the towel and then condense into droplets on the inside of the plastic cover. The drops will run down the inside of the plastic and into the can. The water you collect in the can will be fresh water, because when water evaporates, salt and other minerals in it are left behind.

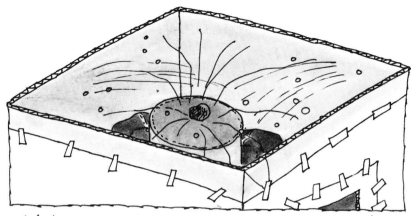

Water evaporates from the towel,
condenses on the plastic and
runs down into the can!

You may find ways to improve this device. You might use a dark towel, for example, or paint the inside of the box black. (Black is a good heat absorber.) Or, you may invent your own style of evaporator. Just remember that your design must do what commercial evaporators do. It must cause salt water to evaporate, it must cause water to condense, and it must collect the fresh water.

The Greek island of Syme is one place that has a commercial solar evaporation unit. Seawater is pumped into long, narrow, shallow channels that are lined with black plastic. The channels are covered with clear plastic. Sun shines through the clear plastic and causes the water to evaporate. The vapor condenses on the underside of the clear plastic and then drains into collectors. Because there are few people on the island, the process furnishes enough water for everyone. If demands were high, solar distillation could not furnish enough water.

Even though sunlight is free, fresh water obtained by solar distillation is not cheap. It costs a lot to install the equipment and to maintain it. Still, on the island of Syme, solar distillation has lowered the cost of water. There is no source of fresh water on

Syme except rainfall. There is very little rainfall, and there are not enough places to store the water even when it does rain. So, the islanders' water had to be brought in from the mainland. Huge plastic tubes—about 30 feet across and 100 feet long—would be filled with fresh water. Since fresh water is lighter than salt water, the tube-tanks floated on top of the sea. Boats towed them to Syme, where the fresh water was pumped into concrete reservoirs. It was a very expensive way to get fresh water!

Reverse Osmosis

Another way of removing salt from water uses osmosis. Osmosis is the process by which liquids can be moved through what is called a semipermeable membrane. (If something is permeable, any liquid or gas will go through it. If something is semipermeable, only certain materials will go through it.)

If you put fresh water on one side of a semipermeable membrane and salt water on the other, the fresh water will move through the membrane into the salt water. Obviously this does not help in purifying water. However, when pressure is applied to the salty water, the water will go through the membrane, leaving the salt behind. Since this is opposite to the normal movement, the process is called *reverse* osmosis. Desalting water in this way has many advantages. The salt water does not have to be heated, so not as much energy is required. The process is simple, so the equipment is not too expensive to build, install, and maintain. And because the water stays cool, the equipment does not corrode too quickly. (Corrosion is a problem in processes in which the water is heated.)

Reverse osmosis removes all minerals from water, not just salt. The process is used to a small extent in the treatment of waste water. One of the places this is done is the island of St. John, in the U.S. Virgin Islands.

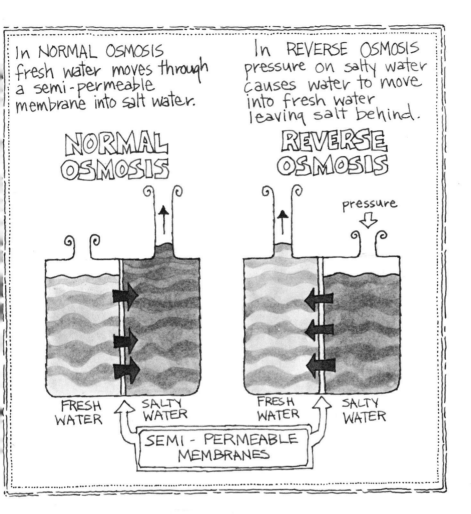

In NORMAL OSMOSIS fresh water moves through a semi-permeable membrane into salt water.

In REVERSE OSMOSIS pressure on salty water causes water to move into fresh water leaving salt behind.

NORMAL OSMOSIS

REVERSE OSMOSIS

pressure

FRESH WATER SALTY WATER FRESH WATER SALTY WATER

SEMI - PERMEABLE MEMBRANES

A large reverse osmosis installation is located in Yuma, Arizona, along the Colorado River. As the river flows over hundreds of miles of rock and sand, it collects salt and many other minerals. At Yuma, the river water is pushed through semipermeable membranes. The salts and minerals in the water are removed, and fresh water is put back into the river. The Yuma desalting plant treats 72 million gallons of water every day, and the cost is rather low. People in seacoast cities who are looking for ways to increase their fresh water supplies will be greatly interested in the Yuma plant.

Icebergs

Most of earth's fresh water is frozen in glaciers in mountainous areas, and in ice caps at the North and South Poles. The water is fresh because ice caps and glaciers are made of snow that has piled up for thousands of years, one layer packed tightly on another, making hard snow-ice. Icebergs are pieces that break off the main glaciers or ice caps and float away, carried along by ocean currents into warmer waters, where they eventually melt. It has been estimated that each year 430 cubic miles of ice become icebergs. That amount of ice would make enough fresh water to fill the annual water needs of five billion people—many more than all the people in the world.

The development of many parts of the world depends upon sufficient amounts of fresh water, and it may come from icebergs. Numerous people, especially in the Arab states and in California, have discussed the possibility of harnessing icebergs and towing them to their harbors. Fresh water from the melting ice could be caught and pumped through the town's water system. If an iceberg ten miles long and 1,000 or more feet thick could be towed

to Los Angeles, it would provide more than a year's supply of water for the city and the surrounding area. To catch the water from the melting ice, a huge, heavy plastic bag would be placed around the iceberg. Pipes inserted into the plastic bag would carry the fresh water to the land and into the water system.

No one has ever actually tried to tow an iceberg to a harbor. For one thing, it would be expensive—ten or 12 tugboats would be needed to move a large iceberg, and the cost for fuel alone would be over 100 million dollars. That's too much, even for the oil-rich Arab countries!

A plan that would cost a fraction of that amount has been suggested. The iceberg would be pushed along by propellers turned by electric motors fastened to the iceberg. The electricity

would come from generators driven by a substance such as ammonia or Freon that evaporates at a low temperature. The substance, heated by the warm sea surrounding the iceberg, would turn to a gas and would drive the turbines. Then the cold temperature of the ice would turn the gas into a liquid. The liquid would then go to a heat exchanger surrounded by seawater; it would be heated and turned in to a gas again, and the cycle would continue. No fuel would be needed to vaporize the liquid, and so to run the generators, so there would be little cost beyond that of the reusable generating system.

Maybe such a system would work. Critics point out that the icebergs would melt as they were being moved, and the generators themselves might then sink into the sea. But perhaps the engines could ride on barges that would be connected by pipes and ropes to the iceberg. The iceberg would certainly melt somewhat during the journey. But even if it was reduced to only one cubic mile, the iceberg would still contain a trillion gallons of water—about a two-year supply for a city the size of New York.

One problem with using icebergs to supply water is that a large iceberg would affect the weather in the area of a city. Air around

the iceberg would be very cold. Warmer air blowing into the region would be cooled, causing water vapor in the air to condense into droplets. Clouds would form, or possibly fogbanks—and these might blow toward the land. The iceberg would have to be placed so the fog would not be undesirable—perhaps some distance from the city.

Using icebergs to supply water to regions that badly need it is an interesting possibility. The self-contained electric generating system that would run the propellers to move an iceberg must be developed. (A test installation is now operating in Hawaii.) And engineers must study the behavior of icebergs. Would they break up as they were moved into warm water? Or, would they perhaps tip over because of changes in balance caused by melting? After scientists learn the answers to these questions, we may see icebergs moved into arid regions of the world—parts of the Arabian Peninsula, California, Africa, and Australia.

3 | Surface Water

Today we usually get water from rivers and lakes, springs and wells—the same sources that have been used down through history. When choosing a source, people try to select one that is close by, one that has enough water to supply everyone in the community, and one that is fresh and more or less free of pollution. That means that rivers and lakes are the most common sources.

Rivers and Lakes

One reason cities are often on rivers—along the Thames in England, the Rhine and the Danube in Europe, the Yellow River in China and so on—is the large supply of fresh water. Obviously, cities built by freshwater lakes (Lake Michigan, for example) are there for the same reason.

People who live by rivers and lakes may not need to build aqueducts and reservoirs. However, people living by rivers may want to build dams. Rivers sometimes dry up during hot summers, or the flow decreases drastically. So dams are sometimes built to hold back the river water and release it as it is needed. This has been done in the Tennessee River, for example, and in the Colorado River. (There the Hoover Dam holds back as much water as would flow in the river during two years.) Dams may also control or prevent flooding—the Aswan Dam on the Nile River in Egypt does this.

Dams are especially important to farmers. In some areas, disastrous flooding used to occur every spring. With dams, floods do not ruin crops. Dams also assure farmers of a steady supply of water for irrigation. With dams, crops may be grown where none could be cultivated before.

Purifying Water

Over the years, many rivers and lakes have become polluted because it is very easy for people to pour sewage and other waste products into them. That is why most cities must now purify the water they take from rivers or lakes.

We might consider London a typical city that obtains its water from a river. Water is pumped from the upper part of the Thames River, and lesser rivers as well, into reservoirs. Here some of the mud and silt settles out. The water then goes into filtering tanks, where finer particles are removed. After chlorine is added to kill bacteria, the water is pumped into other reservoirs close to where the water is to be used. From these reservoirs the water flows through some 9,000 miles of pipes to all parts of the city.

Reservoirs

Although New York City is on the Hudson River, it does not use river water, except during long periods of drought when its system of reservoirs does not furnish enough water. As I said in chapter 1, most of New York City's water comes from the upper part of New York State. An aqueduct carries water 100 miles or more to one of two reservoirs about 30 miles from New York. From there the water goes to another reservoir closer by; then it goes into two pipes some 20 miles long, 10 and 20 feet across and several hundred feet under the surface. These deliver the one and a half billion gallons of water that New Yorkers use every day.

New York's reservoir system serves the city well, though some water is lost through leakage from pipes. Most people in New York, as elsewhere, take their water supply for granted. The amount of water New York City uses could be reduced sharply if people had to pay for water, so they would be more careful with it. New York and London are about the same size, yet New Yorkers use about three times as much water as Londoners.

The water held in reservoirs and in the lakes made by dams is useful in various ways. Man-made lakes and reservoirs can be used for recreation—boating and fishing. Wild animals may drink from them. And when water is released, it may flow through turbines that generate electricity.

Some man-made lakes can be enormous. The Akosombo Dam, on the Volta River in Ghana, produces a lake that is over 250 miles long. It is one of the largest man-made lakes in the world.

Planning Ahead

People who depend upon surface water for their daily supply must plan ahead. Hundreds of years ago, people just took water straight out of rivers and lakes. Today, people may have to connect lakes with large pipes, build reservoirs, hold rivers back with dams. They may need networks of aqueducts, and they almost certainly need systems for purifying their water. It takes a long time to build a modern water system. The first part of New York's system was built 150 years ago, and London's was built before that. A community or area that does not have an adequate water system may suffer greatly in a drought. As we have seen, this happened in northern New Jersey very recently, in 1980–81.

4 | Groundwater

Throughout the world, people obtain water mostly from rivers, lakes, and reservoirs. However, water that is under the ground is also important. In Germany, more than 70 percent of the water supply comes from groundwater; in Israel, this figure is about 54 percent; and in Britain and the United States, it's about 20 percent.

Groundwater might be very near the surface, only 8 or 10 feet under the ground, or it might be down 75 or 100 feet, or even half a mile. Groundwater is water in the cracks and crevices of layers of stone, in spaces between pieces of gravel and between grains of sand. Tremendous amounts of water are stored in this way. There is 30 times more water under the ground than there is in all the world's rivers and lakes.

A glass of sand may help you to understand how this can be. If you fill a glass with dry sand, the glass is full. But you can still put a lot of water into the glass. The water goes into spaces between the sand particles. It's amazing how much water you can add to a glass that is already "full" of dry sand.

This is what happens under the ground. Rain seeps into the ground and fills spaces between grains of sand and bits of gravel; it also seeps into the cracks in rocks. Over the entire earth, the average rainfall is 35 inches a year—some places get a lot less and others get a lot more. About a third of the rain runs off into streams that flow into the oceans. Some rain evaporates back into the air soon after it falls. Large amounts are used almost immediately by plants. But a lot of rainwater goes into the ground. It becomes groundwater.

How Groundwater Forms

Soil lies at the surface of the earth—it holds the roots of trees and plants. As I have said, a lot of the rainwater that falls is used by plants. (It takes about 40 gallons of water to produce every pound of leaves or crops made by a plant.) Some of the water in topsoil evaporates into the air. The rest moves downward to form a groundwater reserve.

As you probably know, the amount of water in the topsoil of an area changes a great deal, depending on the amount of rainfall. When there is a big rainstorm, the amount and weight of the water that falls is amazing. Water is heavy—five gallons weigh about 40 pounds, as you discover when you lift a pail filled with water.

During a heavy storm, when there may be two inches of rainfall, 90 pounds of water fall on each square yard of earth—more than 200 tons on an acre!

The amount of water in a groundwater reserve also depends on rainfall. However, even during long dry spells there will be some water deep below the surface of the earth. The amount of water in an underground reserve doesn't change too much unless the reserve is tapped.

Groundwater does not necessarily stay in one place. If the material below the topsoil is sand and gravel, the water may move several yards in a day—both downward and sideways. If the underground material is shale and clay, water cannot move through easily. It may move only half an inch or so in 24 hours. That groundwater may remain for several years in just about the same place where it first collected. But where sand and gravel underlie the soil, groundwater may travel deep below the surface and then move hundreds of miles from where it entered the ground.

There is some groundwater just about everywhere, even under the Sahara Desert. The water there has traveled thousands of miles from mountains to the north. And it may have taken 30,000 years for those groundwater reserves to accumulate and move in beneath the desert from the rainy regions where the water first

35

entered the ground. Wells to tap the water under the Sahara would have to be so deep that the cost of getting the water out would be much too high. However, in many parts of the world groundwater can be removed inexpensively.

If all the groundwater in the world were pumped to the surface, there would be enough to cover the earth to a depth of 100 feet. But groundwater is not spread evenly around the earth. Some regions have much more than others. We are fortunate, because much of our country has large amounts of groundwater. Every day we use almost 500 billion gallons of water. Much of it comes from lakes and rivers on the surface, but some of it comes from under the ground. In some regions—on Long Island and in the Great Plains states, for example—95 percent of the water comes from wells that tap groundwater supplies.

Groundwater Usage

In many places, groundwater is being used much more rapidly than it can be replaced. That's happening throughout the western United States, and especially in parts of California, Arizona, Texas, and New Mexico. Deep-well pumps run night and day, bringing the water to the surface. There is not enough rainfall in these places to build up new groundwater as fast as the old is being used. In fact, the groundwater in these regions comes from the far-off Rocky Mountains, and it probably took thousands of years for the water to move to the places where it is now being brought out of the ground.

Much of the water in the Great Plains states also comes from the Rocky Mountains. Farmers in this region have been using millions and millions of gallons of groundwater for irrigating their crops. The level of the groundwater in the area is dropping, so people must dig deeper and deeper wells, and spend more and more money, to pump water to the surface.

To be sure groundwater reserves are not drained dry, many communities have had to regulate water usage. Arizona now has statewide water usage regulations. The number of wells in Arizona is limited—no one can dig a new well unless it is registered. The construction of new homes is also limited, and no new farms that need irrigating can be started. The owners of the present farms are told how much water they can pump for their crops. People in cities have also had to reduce their water usage. People building new houses cannot have lawns that need watering, but must land-scape their yards with plants that need little water.

Laws like the ones in Arizona will help the groundwater supply to increase. But recharging groundwater reserves takes a long, long time. Water engineers think that it will be about 250 years before Arizona can reach a balance between the amount of groundwater that is being taken out and the amount that is going in. At present, Arizona is taking out two and a half *million* more acre-feet a year than are being put back into the supply. (An acre-foot of water is the amount needed to cover one acre to a depth of one foot. That's a lot of water, because there are 43,500 square feet in an acre.)

Aquifers

The gravel and sandy or rocky layer that holds groundwater is called an aquifer. The word comes from *aqua,* the Latin word for water, and *-fer,* meaning to give or to yield. The top of an aquifer is called the water table. It is not flat, but tends to have high and low spots that more or less match the hills and valleys of the earth's surface. During dry spells, the water table drops, and it rises during rainy periods. The water table in an area also drops when large amounts of water are pumped out of an aquifer. As I have said, this has happened in Arizona and a number of other places.

Deep aquifers, like the ones that are tapped in Arizona and the Great Plains, are somewhat like a sandwich. The aquifer lies between two layers of clay or solid rock through which water does not move. Water from directly above cannot get into such an aquifer. Even if there were a lot of local rainfall, it would not help to recharge these groundwater reserves. The water in such aquifers came from hundreds of miles away—it moved downward and sideways to its present position.

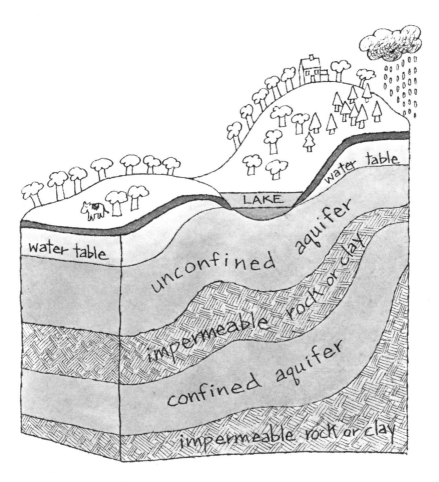

Aquifers are frequently given names to identify them. A water-bearing layer beneath Long Island is called the Magothy aquifer. It is recharged by rainfall. In the western United States, the Ogallala aquifer extends for thousands of square miles from Texas to the Dakotas. Thousands of wells puncture it and remove billions of gallons of water a year. (Most of this water is used for irrigating crops.) The water in the Ogallala aquifer accumulated over thousands of years and moved slowly through rocky layers far below the surface of the earth. Today, wells are mining the Ogallala aquifer dry; the water table is dropping. At the present rate of use, this aquifer will be drained in 20 or 30 years, perhaps sooner. Wells will go dry, and there will be a water disaster in states that have depended upon the Ogallala aquifer for their water supply.

Can people do anything to keep aquifers from running dry? The answer is yes. For one thing, people can use less water. As we've seen, laws in Arizona and other places are aimed at reducing water usage. And there are other ways in which people can help to build up groundwater reserves.

Building Groundwater Supplies

One simple way to help maintain groundwater supplies is to build catch basins. These are man-made ponds that catch rainwater and allow it to seep into the ground slowly. Catch basins reduce runoff—less rainwater flows into streams and rivers and out into the oceans. Still, a large amount of the water caught in catch basins is lost. Some water evaporates into the air, and some is used by plants as soon as it seeps into the ground. Some of the remaining water is held close to the surface of the earth, only a few feet down, so it also evaporates, though slowly.

Stream diversion can also help to build groundwater reserves. Deep pits are dug and the bottoms are covered with sand, or stone quarries are sealed to make gigantic pits. Then pipes or canals carry water from a river or stream into the pit. Since the bottom of the pit is sandy or gravelly, the water seeps downward to become groundwater. Not too much water is lost by evaporation, but people have to be careful not to drain streams and rivers completely dry.

A third way people can help to maintain groundwater reserves is to make efficient use of water-cooled air conditioners.

The temperature of groundwater stays close to the average temperature of the air over a region. This means that in much of the northeastern part of the country, groundwater holds steady at 50 to 60 degrees Fahrenheit all year long. This region has hot summers, so air conditioners are widely used. One way of cooling air is to use cool groundwater. Large buildings use hundreds of thousands of gallons for this purpose.

In years past, the water from air conditioners went into sewers after it was used. Fortunately, it is now returned to the groundwater reserve. Users are required to dig deep holes into which the water goes after it has gone through the air conditioners. The water slowly seeps into the ground and so recharges groundwater supplies.

In some locations, the water from air conditioners pours into shallow ponds or catch basins with sandy bottoms. The water filters through the sand and becomes groundwater again. But deep holes are best for recycling the water, because they have a smaller surface. When water is held in shallow ponds, evaporation is so fast that as much as six inches of depth may be lost in a single season.

Heat Pumps

Because groundwater remains at the same temperature all year round, it may be warmer than air temperatures during the winter months. Heat pumps are devices that use the heat in groundwater for heating buildings.

Heat pumps burn no fuel. The only energy a heat pump requires is the electricity to run the pump. A heat pump is an appliance that moves heat from one place to another in much the same way that a refrigerator does.

Your refrigerator takes heat from the air and the food inside and pushes the heat into the kitchen. Put your hand near the floor along the bottom of the refrigerator while it's running, and you'll feel the heat. In a way, the refrigerator is heating the kitchen at the same time that it's cooling food.

A heat pump heats a building at the same time that it cools groundwater. A pipe carries groundwater to the pump and returns the water to the ground. (No *water* is actually used.) Heat is removed from the groundwater and fans push the heat into the building. The pump concentrates heat. It takes heat from a large amount of groundwater that is at, say, 52 degrees Fahrenheit, and creates enough warmth to raise the temperature of a house to a comfortable 68 to 70 degrees. If the air temperature outside stays very low, the heat pump must run a lot. Even so, it is much cheaper to run the pump than it is to buy oil to burn in an oil furnace.

In summer, the heat pump can reverse. Then it will take heat from inside a building and transfer the heat to the groundwater. The temperature inside a building can be lowered several degrees this way.

HEATING WITH THE HEAT PUMP

heat is removed from water by pump

FAN BLOWS HEAT

groundwater

COOLING WITH THE HEAT PUMP

Pump removes heat from building and returns it to groundwater

groundwater

There have been a few experiments in making groundwater much cooler through the use of heat pumps. In winter, groundwater at, say, 52 Fahrenheit degrees is pumped to the surface and pushed through a heat pump. Then the water goes to a circulator that is exposed to the open air, where the temperature may be only 35 Fahrenheit degrees or so. The water becomes very cold. This very cold water is then put back into the ground, where it remains until summer. The idea is that this extra-cold groundwater will be extra-effective for air-conditioning buildings in the summertime.

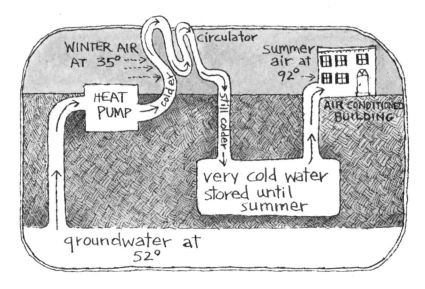

Some people are wary about heat pumps. They say that if they are used widely, the pumps will cool groundwater down so much that plants will not grow well. But this seems unlikely, for plant roots do not reach down to the groundwater levels tapped by heat pumps. Besides, groundwater contains so much heat that only extremely wide use of heat pumps would cause a noticeable change in overall groundwater temperature. At any rate, the good thing about heat pumps is that they do *not* reduce the supply of groundwater. They simply remove heat from it in winter, or add heat to it during the summer months.

5 | Wells, Springs, and Caverns

A well is a hole in the ground that reaches into groundwater. The hole may be only a few inches in diameter, or it may be much wider, perhaps several yards across. In ancient times wells were dug by hand, and they were often 100 feet across and 150 or 200 feet deep. The holes were lined with stones or bricks to keep the sides from caving in. (In those days a well would be considered small if it was only 3 or 4 feet across—just large enough for a man to get into.) When people dug down to a little below the water table, water would flow into the hole and reach as high as the water table. Buckets were lowered into the water and then pulled to the surface. Much later, pumps for removing the water were mounted above wells.

Modern wells are much smaller than those of ancient days. They are not dug, but are made by driving a pipe two or three inches in diameter into the ground. The simplest way to get the pipe into the ground is to pound it in with a heavy hammer. A special machine may drop a heavy weight onto the pipe to drive it down. Sections of pipe are fastened together to make a long, unbroken lining for the well.

Today, wells may also be drilled. This is done when the aquifer being tapped lies below layers of solid rock. A hard steel bit drives and turns, grinding into the rock. As the bit goes deeper, pipe is placed in the hole as a lining.

In many wells, the bottom section of pipe, the one that reaches into the groundwater, is capped with heavy screening. Water can get into the pipe through the holes in the screening, but sand and gravel are filtered out.

To keep supplying water, the pipe lining a well must reach below the water table. Water goes into the pipe and is pumped to the surface. A pipe two or three inches across will furnish enough water for most homes.

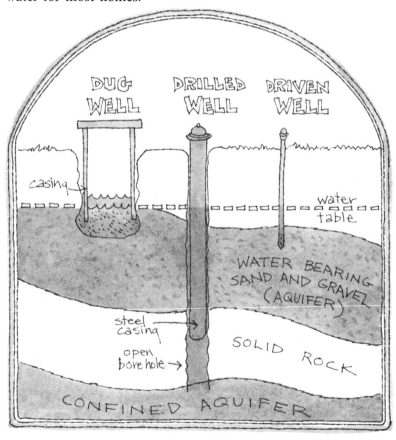

You can get an idea of how water gathers in a well by using wire screening and a glass of sand.

1 Roll a piece of screening around a pencil to make a cylinder.

2 Enlarge the cylinder so it is about ½ inch across and fasten a piece of wire around it to keep it from unrolling.

3 Place the cylinder upright in a glass and then fill the glass with sand, keeping the sand out of the cylinder.

4 Pour water into the sand. The sand will take up the water but the water will also go into the cylinder .... your well.

5 If you removed water from inside the cylinder, additional water would go into it from the sand, but the level of water in your well would be lower than at first.

6 You could raise the level of the water again by pouring more water into the sand.

47

What is happening is that pressure from the water in the sand is pushing some water through the porous screening to fill the empty place in the middle of the glass. In an old-fashioned well, water was pushed into the hole through the spaces between the stones or bricks lining the hole. In a modern well, water pressure pushes water up into the pipe from the bottom. The water in a well never reaches higher than the water table (the top of the aquifer). That is why it usually must be drawn to the surface with pumps or buckets.

Artesian Wells

There is one kind of well in which the water reaches nearly to the surface of the ground—or may even spout above it! That is the artesian well.

To understand artesian wells, we must realize that aquifers do not always lie flat below the surface of the earth—they may be slanted, or inclined. If an inclined aquifer is the "sandwich" kind, with a solid layer of rock or clay both above it and below it, then artesian wells may occur.

An artesian well is always located "downhill" from the top of an inclined aquifer. That is, the well taps a part of the aquifer that is lower than the aquifer's upper end. The pressure of the water in the part of the aquifer "uphill" from the well forces water far up into the well. Because the aquifer is surrounded by solid rock or clay, water cannot move out of the aquifer into other layers of the earth, and this increases the pressure. If pressure is great enough, water will spout above ground level, like a fountain. Artesian wells will stay full for centuries if the groundwater supply is recharged by rainfall in the area at the upper end of the aquifer.

Artesian wells have been known for thousands of years. The

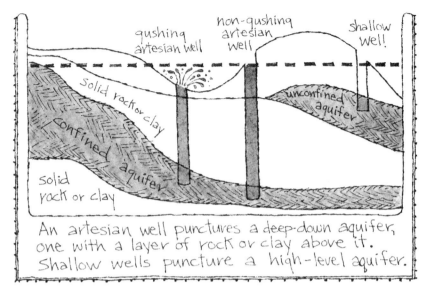

An artesian well punctures a deep-down aquifer, one with a layer of rock or clay above it. Shallow wells puncture a high-level aquifer.

Labels in figure: qushing artesian well; non-qushing artesian well; shallow well; Solid rock or clay; confined aquifer; unconfined aquifer; solid rock or clay

name comes from Artois, a place in France that the Romans called Artesium. There, ancient artesian wells are still used today.

A well provides ample water if the hole reaches an abundant source. However, a well might be a "dry hole"—the hole goes down and down, but no water is found. Or water may flow into the well very slowly, or the well may run dry after a time. Well drillers usually know the area where they are drilling; they know where other wells are located and the amount of water these wells produce. Even so, they sometimes dig dry holes, and have to keep trying other locations until they hit a good water supply.

Water Witching

Some people are convinced that you'll never dig a dry well if you use a water witcher. A water witcher is a person who uses a forked stick or steel "divining rod" to locate groundwater. Some water witchers not only tell you where to dig a well, but also predict how deep the well will have to be, and how much water it will supply. However, most water witchers are not so certain—they merely tell where to dig a well, and leave it at that.

Water witchers, also called water dowsers, may seem to have magic powers. They claim they can find water under the ground even though none of their senses gives them any clue to its presence. A water witcher can't see the water, hear it or smell it, much less touch it or taste it. Not surprisingly, water witchers are not always successful in locating groundwater. A well dug after a water witcher has picked the "right" spot may still be a dry hole.

What a water witcher does is to walk back and forth over the land while holding a forked stick or divining rod in both hands. (Any kind of stick will do, though most water witchers prefer one from a peach, witch hazel, apple, or willow tree.) The two branches of the fork are held firmly, with the palms of the hands up. The third prong of the stick or rod points skyward at an angle of about 45 degrees.

The witcher goes back and forth, back and forth over the property, walking slowly and quietly, holding the stick or rod firmly to the front. Suddenly the stick vibrates and the third prong turns toward the ground. As the witcher continues to walk, the stick rises to its original position. The witcher turns and goes back toward the spot where the stick pointed downward. Once again the stick points to the ground. This is the spot, the water witcher says—this is where the well should be dug.

You might think it is amazing that water would be found where a witcher says a well should be dug. But often water witchers do prove to be good water finders. Of course, many people say you don't need a water witcher to find water. All you need, they say, is a good well man, someone who knows about wells and has experience with them. But others believe water witchers really make a difference. They wouldn't think of drilling a well before calling in a water witcher.

THREE WAYS TO HOLD A DOWSING ROD

1. Palms Down Method
2. Palms Up Method (arms can be crossed or uncrossed)
3. Four Finger Method

Not everyone can "witch" water. But no training is needed to do it. You yourself might be a water witcher. Cut a forked twig from a tree and then try walking over a field while holding it in front of of you. The witching rod may suddenly turn toward the ground. Stories say that sometimes the movement is so strong that bark is stripped off the twig. When you try water witching, be serious. Some witchers concentrate so hard they seem to be in a trance.

Water witchers are also called water dowsers, and what they do is called dowsing. Maybe dowsing *is* a kind of magic, or maybe dowsers have a special "sixth sense" that reacts to water and makes the forked stick move. Or perhaps a dowser just knows the spots in an area where water is most likely to be found. In any case, dowsing has been around for a long time, and is still important to many people seeking sources of groundwater.

51

Springs

You don't always have to drill a well to get groundwater. At certain locations, usually on hillsides, an aquifer may break the surface and water may flow out of the ground, making a spring. The spring may be very small—only a foot or so across—and the flow may be slight. But in some places the amount of water flowing from a spring is amazing. At Thousand Springs, Idaho, springs extend along the surface for almost a mile, and 600,000 gallons of water flow from them every day. At Silver Springs in Florida, the flow is even greater—nearly a million gallons a day.

Such tremendous amounts of water from springs is unusual. More often the flow is small and unsteady. Flow usually varies with the amount of rainfall, and it is seldom that a spring can supply enough water for a village or town.

Caves and Caverns

Groundwater occurs at various levels. Sometimes it is very deep under the surface. But at other locations groundwater is contained in topsoil that lies above solid rock. This water may gradually seep down deeper and deeper through little cracks in the rock. If it moves through limestone, the water may eventually create huge caves and caverns.

When rain falls, some of the carbon dioxide that is in the air dissolves in the water. When water and carbon dioxide combine, a weak acid is formed. This acid is strong enough to dissolve limestone. So, as groundwater moves slowly through tiny cracks in limestone, it removes some of the limestone—and over the years the cracks become wider. Eventually, caverns develop along the cracks in layers of limestone. Such caverns may be little more than enlarged cracks, or they may be huge open areas as large as a soccer field. Perhaps you have visited spectacular caverns, such as the Howe Caverns in New York State, the Shenandoah and Luray Caverns in Virginia, Mammoth Cave in Kentucky, and the Carlsbad Caverns in New Mexico.

The water that drips through the cracks in limestone may collect in an underground lake at the bottom of a cavern. And sometimes a stream may flow through the cavern. Such a stream may flow underground for several hundred yards or even several miles before it flows out of a hillside and then into an aboveground stream.

At ground level, there may be deep holes along the course of an underground stream. These are called sinkholes. They result when part of the roof of a cavern caves in, or when the acid in groundwater eats a hole straight down through the rock below the topsoil.

Stalactites and Stalagmites

Inside many limestone caverns stony "icicles" hang from the roof. They are formed when water drips slowly out of the limestone. It drips so slowly that carbon dioxide has time to leave the water, and calcium carbonate is left. Then, when the water evaporates, a bit of the mineral calcite is left on the roof of the cavern. With each drip of water a bit more calcite builds up on the roof, and the icicle begins to take shape. It starts out as a hollow tube.

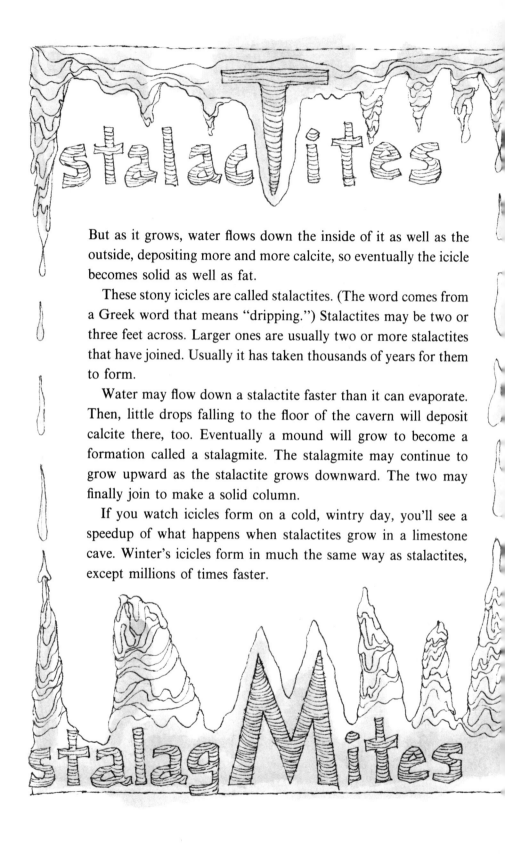

Stalactites

But as it grows, water flows down the inside of it as well as the outside, depositing more and more calcite, so eventually the icicle becomes solid as well as fat.

These stony icicles are called stalactites. (The word comes from a Greek word that means "dripping.") Stalactites may be two or three feet across. Larger ones are usually two or more stalactites that have joined. Usually it has taken thousands of years for them to form.

Water may flow down a stalactite faster than it can evaporate. Then, little drops falling to the floor of the cavern will deposit calcite there, too. Eventually a mound will grow to become a formation called a stalagmite. The stalagmite may continue to grow upward as the stalactite grows downward. The two may finally join to make a solid column.

If you watch icicles form on a cold, wintry day, you'll see a speedup of what happens when stalactites grow in a limestone cave. Winter's icicles form in much the same way as stalactites, except millions of times faster.

Stalagmites

Geodes

Stalactites and stalagmites are made when water loses calcium carbonate that has been dissolved in it. Geodes, stones with crystals inside of them, are formed when water loses dissolved silica, or sand. Water is often called the universal solvent. That means water will dissolve just about everything, even sand, although the action may be very slow.

Silica-laden water moving through a crack in a rock may reach a small opening where the silica is deposited. Gradually, more and more silica collects, and it forms crystals called quartz. (Salt will crystalize out of water in much the same manner. You can see this happen if you dissolve a teaspoonful of salt in half a glass of water and then let the mixture stand so the water evaporates.) If the silica is deposited rapidly, very small crystals will be formed—in fact, they'll be so small you cannot see them. They will combine to make the colored bands of a substance called agate. But if the silica is deposited slowly, the crystals will be much larger. They may fill the inside of a rounded or irregular cavity in a rock, and the rock then is a geode. The quartz crystals may be two or three inches long, and sometimes they are even larger. They may be clear, or they may be white, pink, red, violet, or green. Rock collectors prize geodes because of the spectacular crystals in them.

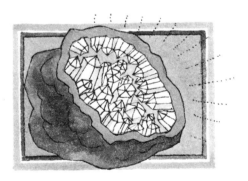

6 | Water Pollution

All the water in the world is used water, so there are many ways the water could have picked up impurities—many ways it could have become polluted.

The droplets of water that make the clouds are the purest water that occurs naturally. However, as droplets grow into drops and fall to earth, the rain picks up some impurities. Near the ocean, salt from sea spray is added to it. Over farm regions and deserts, dust is added. Carbon dioxide and other gases in the atmosphere dissolve in rainwater. And as soon as the rain reaches land, many other substances may dissolve in it. Some of them are iron, calcium, magnesium, sodium, potassium, chlorides, sulfates, and nitrates. Most of them remain in the water as it flows into rivers and lakes, or as it seeps into the ground. Groundwater can often be used without being treated at all. Because it has been filtered through the soil, groundwater is purer than the water in most lakes and rivers. However, it may still contain impurities that it picked up on its way into the ground, or minerals that have dissolved out of rocks.

Hard Water

When water contains dissolved minerals, it is said to be hard. Soap added to hard water makes few suds; the action of the soap is destroyed and a scum or curd forms. (In soft water—water containing few if any minerals—very little soap is needed to make a rich lather.) Hard water leaves a stonelike scale in a teakettle, and this scale also forms inside pipes.

When the minerals in water are calcium bicarbonate and magnesium bicarbonate, the water is "temporarily hard." Boiling will remove all but a trace of the bicarbonates. But sulfates of calcium and magnesium make permanent hard water—these minerals are very difficult to remove. Usually permanent hard water is treated with a commercial water softener to remove the minerals.

Rainwater is very soft because it contains no minerals. You can get an idea of how hard your water is if you compare it with rainwater. Collect some rainwater in a nonmetallic container. Put a drop of liquid soap in a bottle of the rainwater. Shake it to make suds. Place a drop of soap in another, identical bottle filled with tap water, and shake the bottle. Compare the two for the amount of suds produced, and for how long the suds remain.

Most groundwater is fairly hard. Its exact hardness will depend upon the kind of rocks that lie under the surface in a particular area. But even very hard groundwater is usually potable—that is, pure enough for people to drink.

Salty Groundwater

Sometimes sodium chloride—ordinary salt—is found in groundwater. The salt may dissolve out of rocks, or it may come from seawater. Salty groundwater is definitely *not* potable!

Towns along the seacoast in the Netherlands, Japan, California, and Long Island often have problems with what is called saltwater intrusion. When excess amounts of water are pumped out of the ground, the water table drops. If it drops below sea level, salt water gets into the groundwater supply. Then old wells cannot be used—they must be abandoned, and new wells drilled further inland.

People have learned that the effects of saltwater intrusion can be reversed. In many coastal areas, freshwater aquifers slope seaward. This means that the natural movement of underground water in the area is seaward, rather than landward. If the water table drops a great deal—and this will happen if people pump out lots of groundwater—the aquifer may no longer slope seaward. Then saltwater intrusion will occur. But if the aquifer is built up again—with fresh water—the salty water will be pushed back out to sea and old wells will once again be usable.

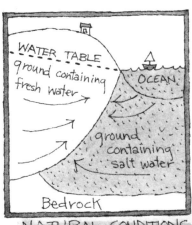

NATURAL CONDITIONS

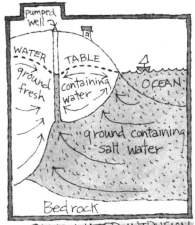

SALT WATER INTRUSION

When wells pump out too much water, salt water may enter the fresh water area.

Rainfall alone can usually build a freshwater aquifer back up—but it might take many years, even decades. So people help speed up the process. They use catch basins. They channel small streams through a series of ponds, so runoff is slowed down and some of the water from the streams has a chance to soak into the ground. In some parts of Long Island, fresh water from streams, ponds, and catch basins is poured down wells, directly into the aquifer.

Modern science has contributed in one way to the process of putting water back into aquifers. In sections of Australia where water is especially scarce, people now spray a film of plastic over the surfaces of their ponds and catch basins. This slows down the loss of water by evaporation into the air.

Saltwater intrusion teaches us a lesson: keeping the water table as high as possible is important! Wise people will take no more water from the ground than rainfall can replace.

Salt can get into groundwater in ways you wouldn't suspect. In many northeastern states, salt is spread on roads during icy weather. As the ice melts, salt is carried into the ground. In New England, salt has seeped into many wells near the roads. Salt for use on roads can also pollute groundwater in the area where it is stored. Great piles of it are held for winter use. When it rains, salt washes from the heap and into the ground.

The very salty water in solar ponds may become a new source of pollution. A solar pond is a shallow man-made reservoir that is lined with leakproof rubber or plastic. Very salty water is put into the pond. Solar energy heats the salt water. Then the heat is collected and used to heat gases that drive electric generators. Solar ponds are now operating in Israel. Test ponds are being built near the Salton Sea in California and the Great Salt Lake in Utah. The danger with solar ponds is that leaks might develop in their "leakproof" linings, and the very salty water would then seep into fresh groundwater reserves.

Man-Made Impurities

During the last few decades we have been putting chemicals into the water that cannot be filtered out or otherwise removed. At present some 50,000 chemicals are on the market, and the government has identified 35,000 of them as being hazardous to health. It is staggering to think about the amounts of chemicals produced. In the 1940s, industry had produced one billion barrels of synthetic (man-made) chemicals; at the start of the 1980s the figure had grown to 350 billion barrels!

These chemicals are essential for making all sorts of medicines and thousands of different kinds of plastics, for making food additives, fabrics, and scores of other products that improve our way of life. But whenever chemicals are produced, there are waste products. And a major problem in the world today is what to do with these waste products. Where do you put them?

For decades, chemical wastes were poured into lakes and rivers. Obviously, this polluted those lakes and rivers. More recently, wastes have been put in man-made lagoons. Laws are being passed to eliminate such lagoons, but there are still several thousand of them. Water evaporates from the lagoons, and the chemical wastes become more and more concentrated. The lagoons have sand or dirt bottoms, so the chemicals slowly seep down into the ground—and into groundwater.

Often, once chemicals get into groundwater they cannot be gotten out again. In many cases, groundwater does not move. It may remain for centuries at a single location. Groundwater that moves is purified by the natural filtering action of soil, but impurities remain if the water does not move. Then too, there is little evaporation deep underground. As we learned in chapter 1, water leaves impurities behind when it evaporates—but impurities remain when there is no evaporation.

At the surface of the earth, sunlight helps to purify water. But there is no sunlight deep underground to help purify polluted groundwater.

Sometimes it is possible to treat polluted groundwater to make it safe. Then the water may be pumped to the surface, treated, and put back into the ground. But this is an expensive process. It would be better not to pollute the groundwater in the first place!

People unwittingly pollute water in lots of ways. Here are some examples:

Phosphates cause the foaming action in washing powders. When clothes are washed and rinsed, the phosphates go into the water supply. Years ago, the phosphates reappeared as foam on lakes and ponds in many parts of the country, and people got foaming water when they turned on their faucets. The phosphates were still in the water! There was only one thing to do—stop using the soaps that contained phosphates. So, soaps with phosphates in them were outlawed in many areas—none could be sold at all. People found they could get along very well without phosphates, and the water supply improved. The foaming tap water scared people and made them realize that our water supply is fragile— what we do (or don't do) can affect it greatly.

Chemicals and bacteria from feedlots where cattle are fattened for market often seep into the ground. A ten-acre feedlot with 1,000 cattle produces as much waste as a town of 6,000 people. Rain carries nitrates and bacteria from these wastes into lakes, streams, and groundwater reserves. And the effect of the pollution can continue long after the feedlot has closed down. In North Dakota, the water supply of a village was still contaminated 40 years after a feedlot was closed.

Farmers who use chemicals to prevent plant diseases and to control insects also contribute to water pollution. Tons and tons of the chemicals are sprayed on crops. When it rains, some of the chemicals are carried into streams, or they move deep down into the soil. Then they show up in drinking water. Most of the chemicals do not affect people, or they can be treated to make them harmless. But occasionally a harmful chemical cannot be treated, or it turns into an even *more* harmful substance once it combines with water.

In Maine, the spruce budworm has been destroying thousands of acres of pine trees, a crop that the paper industry depends upon. Airplanes fly over the forests spreading a chemical that controls the worms. But the chemical also goes into lakes and ponds, where it harms fish and other life; and the chemical has been found in groundwater.

On Long Island, many wells were contaminated with a poison that came from chemicals used to control insects on potato farms. (Long Island has lots of potato farms.) There wasn't very much poison present, but enough so that people could not safely drink the water. Groundwater could be used for toilets and showers, but all water for drinking and cooking had to be brought in. Eventually, the company that made the chemical installed special filters in all the affected homes. These make the polluted water drinkable, but the people are not pleased, for the filters do not solve the basic problem.

Chemicals used to control insects and plant diseases are not the only ones that pollute water. Chemical fertilizers may get into our water supplies, too. And farmers aren't the only ones who use chemical fertilizers—many people use them on their lawns. Where houses are close together and people use a lot of fertilizer, groundwater often becomes polluted. So, in many areas, the size of lawns is now limited. Building lots may be large, but people must have trees and other plants on most of the lot. Only a small plot can be grassy lawn.

Handling Chemical Wastes

We'll continue to use chemicals in manufacturing, for fertilizers and pesticides, and in thousands of other products. But we must find ways to keep chemicals and chemical wastes out of fresh water, whether that water is in lakes, in rivers, or in the ground.

It is all too easy to dispose of chemical wastes improperly. Here is an example of the kind of thing that can happen:

Love canal was built near Niagara Falls, but it was never used for its intended purpose. Eventually chemicals from a factory were poured into the canal, and then it was covered with a layer of soil. Later, a school and over 100 houses were built along the canal. Decades later, dangerous chemicals seeped into the cellars of the houses and many people became very sick. The situation was so bad that the government moved many of the people out of the area.

It might seem safe to dispose of chemicals by putting them in steel barrels. This has been done in the past. The barrels are dumped all over the country, many times in out-of-the-way places. (In some locations there are thousands of them piled one on top of the other.) The trouble is that gradually the chemicals eat holes in the barrels, or the barrels rust and develop leaks. Then a mixture of chemicals that may contain arsenic and other equally powerful poisons oozes out and into the ground.

The people who live near Grandview, Idaho, have found one answer to the problem of what to do with chemical wastes. In Grandview, some 12 million gallons of chemical wastes have been put into a Titan missile silo. It's unlikely that the chemicals will leak out. The silo is a hole 160 feet deep with concrete walls six feet thick and a concrete floor that is 13 feet thick. However, even huge dumps like this fill up eventually. Other ways to get rid of dangerous chemical wastes must be found.

For quite some time, European countries have been burning

chemical wastes far out at sea. A ship built for the purpose contains large incinerators (burners) that operate at very high temperatures. When chemical wastes are burned, gases are given off; these go into the atmosphere. But there are no towns or villages close by. By the time the gases reach the shore, they have dispersed so much that they are harmless. Often they cannot even be detected.

Very little ash is left after the burning. What ash there is is dumped overboard from the incinerator ship. All the while, the water around the ship is carefully tested to make sure it is not becoming polluted, and that plankton (microscopic food for fish) is not being destroyed.

The *Vulcanus,* one of the European incinerator ships, came over to the Gulf of Mexico for testing. Wastes containing chlorides, substances that form dangerous acids when they are mixed with water, were burned. But no harmful effects to either the water or the atmosphere could be seen. It's expected that incinerator ships of our own will be built in the future, to burn off certain kinds of chemical waste products.

Today, some chemical companies are doing a very sensible thing. They are reducing wastes by finding ways to separate one "waste" chemical from another. The chemicals can then be reused, or they may be sold to other companies. It often happens that one factory can use chemicals that another would have just thrown away.

Sometimes, chemical wastes cannot be recycled, incinerated, or disposed of by other usual methods. (This is true of radioactive wastes, such as those produced by nuclear ships and submarines, and by nuclear generating plants.) What can people do with these wastes?

Such materials can be concentrated and then sealed inside containers made of glass or ceramics (hard pottery). Unlike metal containers, those made of glass or pottery do not corrode. Once filled and sealed, the containers can be put into deep underground caves, perhaps 600 feet below the surface, where they might remain forever.

Those opposed to this plan say that there could be earthquakes that would break open the caves and the ceramic containers. Material inside of them would then pollute the air and water.

In making decisions about such matters, the good points must be weighed against the bad ones—advantages against disadvantages. While earthquakes are possible, the chances are slim that they would occur at any of the carefully selected storage sites. And if an earthquake did occur, the chances that a container would burst open are also very slim. If we want the advantages of technology, we must face the problems that go with it. All things considered, many people believe storage inside ceramics in stable underground caves would be safe for centuries, if not forever.

Other Waste Materials

Chemical wastes from factories are not the only ones that can pollute our water supplies. Ordinary household trash and garbage have water-soluble chemicals in them. Some of those chemicals can be poisonous. Here's what can happen:

Every village and town generates tons and tons of garbage. Often this garbage is put in a town dump and soil is bulldozed over it to make a landfill. For a few years this way of getting rid of garbage works very well. It may even be all right for decades. But after 40 or 50 years, a town may be in real trouble. Rain falling on the landfill washes hundreds of different chemicals out of the trash. Over the decades, the chemicals seep into the ground, and often they reach an aquifer that underlies the region. If the townspeople get their water from wells that tap the aquifer, they are faced with a polluted water supply. In many cases the only way to solve the problem is to pipe water in from a location far enough away to be unaffected by drainage from the landfill.

You might think, from reading this, that all landfills should be banned. However, it is possible to build a landfill that is quite safe for most kinds of waste. The site for such a landfill would have a thick layer of clay above the groundwater level.

To build the landfill, pipes with holes on one side of them are laid on top of the clay, the holes facing up. The pipes lead to a lagoon that has clay sides and a clay bottom so water cannot leak out. (Remember, water does not move through clay.) Garbage is piled on top of the pipes. When it rains, water seeps through the garbage into the pipes, and it is carried to the lagoon.

Because of the clay under the pipes, chemicals from the garbage cannot seep down to the groundwater level. And the water that is carried to the lagoon can be treated to purify it. The water is sprayed into the air to mix it with oxygen. Chlorine (to kill bacteria) will be added as needed, and the water may also be filtered through sand beds. The pure water may then be used to recharge groundwater supplies (as discussed on page 59), or it may go into a lake to become part of the natural water cycle.

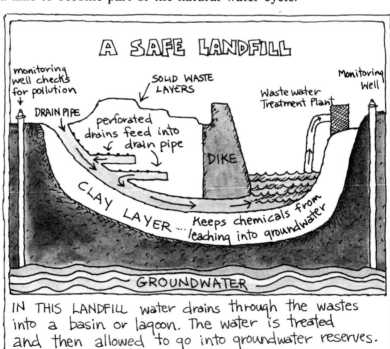

A SAFE LANDFILL

monitoring well checks for pollution

DRAIN PIPE

SOLID WASTE LAYERS

perforated drains feed into drain pipe

DIKE

Waste water Treatment Plant

Monitoring Well

CLAY LAYER ... keeps chemicals from leaching into groundwater

GROUNDWATER

IN THIS LANDFILL water drains through the wastes into a basin or lagoon. The water is treated and then allowed to go into groundwater reserves.

Some household trash does not need to go to a landfill—it can be recycled. Maybe you have helped to collect newspapers or aluminum cans to sell to factories that can reuse them. Paper, aluminum, glass, steel, and other metals all can be recycled.

You can "recycle" other kinds of garbage, too. Organic wastes such as orange peels, coffee grounds, and carrot tops (just about everything but meat and fish) can be put outside in a heap with dead leaves, grass clippings and soil. Soon the materials deteriorate into compost, a rich natural fertilizer that is good to use on lawns, flowers, vegetable gardens, and shrubs.

Some communities now burn trash that cannot be recycled. The heat is used to generate electricity. It seems a perfect solution—you get rid of the trash and turn it into something valuable. Unfortunately, the trash often gives off dangerous gases when it is burned, so ways must be found to trap the gases. There are always a few ashes left that must be disposed of. And when burning isn't complete, the incinerators give off bad odors. But if it is done properly, burning is a good way to get rid of trash.

Space Garbage

If we do not dispose of wastes on our own planet, then we must dispose of them elsewhere. This means they must be sent to the moon, or into space. It has been suggested that certain wastes should be packed into barrels and then loaded aboard rockets that will shoot them far out beyond earth. The barrels would be put into orbit around our planet, where they would remain forever. By using more energy, the wastes could be put into orbit around the sun—or even shot into the sun. It's also conceivable that the containers could be shot out of the solar system into space between the stars.

The cost would be very high—fuel alone would cost an unreasonable amount. People who believe the plan is possible say that the cost could be decreased by using a space shuttle vehicle to carry the wastes into low earth orbit. Then smaller engines that burn very little fuel could put the containers into solar orbit. This could be done. But many people believe we shouldn't consider such a plan, even if it could be done at a reasonable cost. It's unwise, they say, to pollute outer space—and that is what we would be doing. We should concentrate our energy on reducing wastes, they say, and keep those that still accumulate right here on our own planet. In space we'd have no control over them. Here on earth we might eventually find ways to make them safe and reusable.

Acid Rain

Acid rain, a kind of water pollution, is a serious problem in the northeastern United States and in eastern Canada.

Lemon juice, which is sour, is an acid; so is vinegar. All acids are sour, and the stronger the acid, the more sour it is. We often think of acids as unpleasant. (Very few people would want to drink a glass of vinegar!)

All rainwater contains carbonic acid, so all rain is somewhat acid. But carbonic acid is a very weak acid. If it is the only acid in rain, the rain is normal, and does no harm. But in some places the rain that falls into lakes and ponds is so acid it is killing the fish and other life (frogs, salamanders, toads). When all the life in a lake disappears, we say that the lake has died. There are many dead lakes in New England, New York, and eastern Canada. In West Virginia, too, many fish have been killed by acid rain. Acid rain originates in areas where there are many factories and automobiles.

Rainfall becomes strongly acid because factories and cars put nitrogen oxides and sulfur into the air. When water combines with sulfur dioxide, sulfuric acid forms. And when it combines with nitrogen oxides, nitric acid is created. Both are very strong acids.

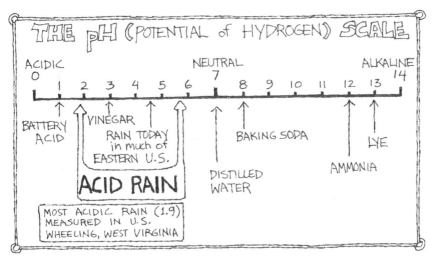

Prevailing Winds

SULFUR + WATER = SULFURIC ACID

NITROGEN OXIDES + WATER = NITRIC ACID

Most of the sulfur that produces acid rainfall seems to come from coal-burning factories and electric generators in the Ohio River Valley. (Some sulfur, but not as much, comes from oil-burning factories and generators in the area.) The sulfur goes up chimneys, is picked up by the wind and is carried 1,000 miles and more. However, these factories are not the only source of acid rain, for dead lakes have been found in parts of the world besides North America. No matter where coal is burned—in Europe, China, Japan, Russia—sulfur put into the air adds to the acid rain problem.

Today, in the United States, new factories have to ensure that sulfur will not go up their chimneys and into the air. It's the law. But factories in some other parts of the world are not regulated.

Nitrogen oxides in the air come mainly from automobiles; these oxides are produced when gasoline is burned in car engines. There are so many cars in the world today that you might think *all* rain would contain nitric acid! Fortunately, engineers are now working to find ways to reduce air pollution by cars.

Some people believe that unless we take drastic steps, acid rain will continue to fall. They insist we must develop kinds of energy that put *no* wastes into the air. Some believe that solar energy is the answer; others feel that nuclear fusion would be more productive. One thing is sure—the world must reduce the amount of acid in rainfall. Dead lakes may be the first stage of disaster, a warning of what could happen all over the world.

7 | Sewage Disposal

A special source of water pollution is sewage—wastes from toilets. It is organic material combined with living bacteria. (Today, sewage also contains detergents from washing machines and from the kitchen.) Disposing of sewage and returning purified water to the water supply is a problem people have faced all through history.

Cities and towns along rivers and on the seacoast used to discharge sewage directly into the water. Some of them still do. But most of those communities now have sewage treatment plants. The sewage goes into a tank where heavy particles (such as sand and gravel) settle to the bottom. The sewage water is then pumped into sedimentation tanks, where smaller bits of solid material settle to the bottom as sludge. But dissolved substances in the sewage water still must be removed. So it is sprayed over beds of gravel. Microscopic bacteria live on the gravel. As the sewage water drips through the gravel, the bacteria remove the dissolved material.

By now the water is quite pure. It is tested, and if it is pure enough it goes into a river or lake. Or it might go into a lagoon, from which it will slowly seep into the ground.

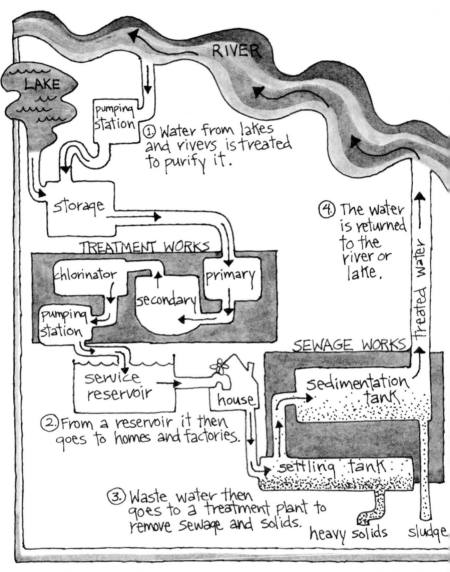

RIVER

LAKE

pumping station

① Water from lakes and rivers is treated to purify it.

storage

TREATMENT WORKS

chlorinator

secondary

primary

pumping station

④ The water is returned to the river or lake.

Treated water

SEWAGE WORKS

service reservoir

house

Sedimentation tank

② From a reservoir it then goes to homes and factories.

settling tank

③ Waste water then goes to a treatment plant to remove sewage and solids.

heavy solids   sludge

Often the sludge goes into another tank, where bacteria break it down. In the process, methane gas is produced. This can be burned to provide heat for the community. After the bacteria work on it, some of the sludge still remains. This can be dried and then sold as compost—farmers can put it on their fields, and people can use it on their gardens.

Septic Systems

In rural areas where town sewage systems don't exist, sewage goes from houses into septic tanks or cesspools.

A septic tank is a large concrete cylinder or box that is buried under the ground. Waste water from the house carries sewage into the tank. Bacteria in the sewage break down the organic material. They reduce much of the sewage to liquid. The liquid builds up until it reaches drains through which it flows from the tank.

From the septic tank, the liquid goes into an absorption field. This is a rather large dug-out area that is partly filled with gravel. Pipes with holes in them are laid in the field. The liquid from the septic tank flows into these pipes and then slowly seeps out of them, going through the gravel and then into the soil below.

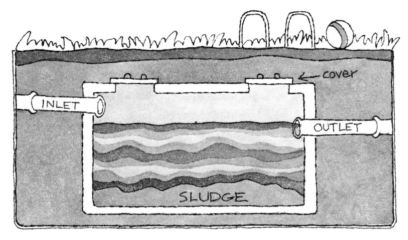

The liquid that leaves the tank still has dissolved wastes in it. Some of them are filtered out as the water goes through the soil, and some are "digested" by bacteria in the soil. Unfortunately, some materials—such as phosphates in detergents—are not broken down by soil or bacteria. They remain in the water and can reappear in wells. As we saw in the last chapter, many communities have had to ban detergents with phosphates in them.

A cesspool is a somewhat simpler form of septic tank. The cesspool is a large concrete tank, eight or ten feet across and six or eight feet high, that has openings all around it. The tank is set into the ground, and gravel is poured all around it. Sewage is treated in the cesspool just as it is treated in the septic tank— bacteria break it down. Water with some dissolved wastes still in it then goes through the openings in the tank and into the gravel that surrounds the tank. The water gradually goes into the soil and down to the groundwater level.

Needless to say, septic systems must be located far from wells. And two tanks cannot be close to each other—there must be a large area of soil all around a tank through which the treated water can move. However, some large communities do treat water with septic systems not much different from those used in rural areas.

The liquid from a septic system that serves a whole community does not go directly into the ground. Instead, the waste water from the tank is pumped into lagoons with impermeable (solid) bottoms. There bacteria, sunlight, and air help to purify the water. Sometimes the lagoons contain green algae that further break down waste materials in the water, and destroy harmful bacteria. After 30 days, chlorine is added to the water to kill any remaining bacteria. Then the water may be pumped up a hillside into a pond with a sandy bottom, so the water can go back into the ground. Or the water may go into lakes and ponds stocked with fish.

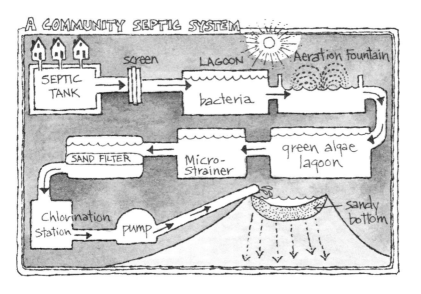

A COMMUNITY SEPTIC SYSTEM

Closed-System Recycling

All water is recycled—it is used over and over, and has been ever since water first formed on our planet. The recycling is usually done naturally, as we saw in chapter 1. But sometimes people choose to recycle water through a special, man-made system called a closed system.

The closed system is used in rural places where homes are built on land so rocky or full of clay that cesspools or septic tanks cannot drain properly. Or the homes might be built where there is very little water, or where it would be very expensive to dig a well because groundwater lies under so much solid rock.

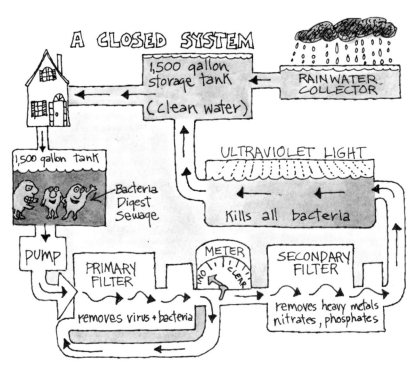

In a closed system, sewage and waste water from the house go into a 1,500-gallon tank. There bacteria "digest" the sewage. Automatic controls turn on pumps at the right time to move the water through a highly effective filtering system that removes most of these bacteria and any viruses that might be in the water. Then the water passes through a meter that measures how clear it is. If additional filtering is needed, the water is directed back through the system. Otherwise it goes to a second filter that removes heavy metals (such as zinc or lead), nitrates, and phosphates from the water. And finally, the water passes through a tank that is bathed in ultraviolet light—the part of sunlight that kills bacteria. The light is strong enough to kill 100 percent of the bacteria in the water. If the system is not functioning properly, there are automatic controls to correct the operation.

After all this treatment, the water goes into another 1,500-gallon tank, where it is stored till it is needed. It is now pure drinking water. The system is completely closed—the people in the house use the same water over and over again. Rainwater is collected and is used to replace the small amount of water that escapes the system through normal leakage and evaporation.

8 | Earth Is a Spaceship

When astronauts went to the moon, their Apollo spacecraft contained food, air, and water—everything the men needed to stay alive. But the amounts were limited; there was no way of getting more of anything. So some materials were reused. Waste products such as water and carbon dioxide were removed from exhaled air, and the air was then recycled. Waste water was filtered and purified and then reused. In a spaceship, sewage could not be recycled. But in a permanent space colony, it would be. Bacteria would be removed and the remaining material would be used as fertilizer for crops.

In many ways, earth is a spaceship in orbit around the sun. There is a certain amount of air on our ship, and a certain amount of water. Both materials are essential if life is to continue. So we must learn to use these resources with care.

It should be no hardship for each of us to use less water. By thinking about water usage, we can easily reduce our daily needs by half. Here are some of the ways *you* can save water:

SAVE

Take a three minute shower. Get wet. Turn off the shower while lathering. Then rinse quickly. Use a timer.

If you have a shower, don't take baths. A bath takes about 25 gallons of water.

25 GALLONS!

5 GALLONS PER FLUSH!

Flush the toilet less often.

3 GALLONS PER MINUTE!

When you wash your face or hands, do it in one minute or less.

30 GALLONS PER LOAD!

Run the washing machine only when there is a full load.

WATER!

Do not run water to cool it. Put a jug of drinking water in the refrigerator.

When you only need a small amount of hot water don't run the water until it gets hot.

Fix a leaky faucet. 20 gallons can leak in a day.

Heat some water in a kettle.

Whenever possible save rinse water and put it to some good use. For example, put it on plants in the garden or use it to wash the dog.

Fill a plastic bottle with water and stand it in the toilet tank. The toilet will use less water but will work just as well because a toilet operates on the LEVEL of the water in the tank, not the AMOUNT. (Don't use bricks — they are apt to crumble and clog pipes)

85

Long ago, when there were few people on our planet, and fewer industries, only small amounts of wastes were produced. The water cycle was sufficient to remove the wastes and to repurify both the air and the water.

Now there are a lot more people, a lot more industries, and a lot more pollutants. Each one of us is important in the struggle to keep our water supply unpolluted. Sensible, controlled use of fertilizers by farmers is important; discharge of waste from factories must be regulated; and wastes of all kinds must be reduced. Our goal should be to use less, and to recycle what we do use. Just as astronauts in spaceships must use their resources with care, so must people on spaceship earth. Our planet contains plenty of water for all our needs, but it will continue to be available only if it is used wisely.

Further Reading

Index

Further Readings

Canby, T. Y. "Water: Our Most Precious Resource." *National Geographic,* August 1980 (158:144–79).

Davis, Kenneth and Leopold, Luna. *Water.* Silver Burdett, 1970.

Hendrey, G. R. "Acid Rain and Gray Snow." *Natural History,* February 1981 (90:58–65).

Keogh, Carol. *Water Fit to Drink.* Rodale Press, 1980.

La Bastille, A. "Acid Rain: How Great a Menace." *National Geographic,* November 1981 (160:652–81).

McLaughlin, D. T. "Water, Water—Where?" *Time,* September 17, 1979 (114:59).

Melne, Lores and Margery. *Water and Life.* Atheneum, 1964.

Reisner, M. "Are We Headed for Another Dust Bowl?" *Reader's Digest,* May 1981 (118:87–92).

Vogt, Evan and Hyman, Ray. *Water Witching U.S.A.* University of Chicago Press, 1979.

Write for information booklets to the Department of Geology or the Water Conservation Department of your state.

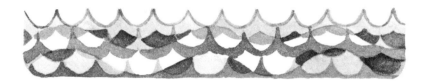

Index

93

95